TODAY'S GOOD NEWS

General Editor: The Rev. David Field
Consulting Editors: The Rev. Dr John Stott
The Rev. Dr Leighton Ford

The Man who had Everything

In the same series

The Man who had Everything

Job

DAVID COOK

Illustrated by Annie Vallotton

Collins/Fount Paperbacks

Church Pastoral Aid Society
Falcon Books

First published in Fount Paperbacks 1978
Text © E. D. Cook 1978
Illustrations © Collins/Falcon Books
Good News Bible, Today's English Version:
Old Testament © American Bible Society,
New York, 1976

British usage edition reproduced here by kind
permission of the British & Foreign Bible Society

Made and printed in Great Britain by
William Collins Sons & Co. Ltd, Glasgow

CONTENTS

Some of the words in the text are printed in **bold type.** This means that they come from the Bible itself.

Before we start . . .

Job's story is like a magnet. Philosophers and poets have written millions of words about it, and ordinary people are drawn to it. It raises questions about right and wrong, reward and punishment, happiness and misery. These are all things that affect each one of us. We have to face the world and understand our experiences. And Job's example can guide us. We certainly need all the help we can get!

The story itself is a very old one. It appears in many different forms. The Egyptians knew about a man like Job. So did the Babylonians and the Sumerians. They all tell stories about his misfortunes. Innocent people do suffer in this world, but no one really understands why. The Book of Job deals with that kind of problem. However, the story has a more basic theme. It looks at the relationship between God and man, and it asks what God is really like.

The experts do not know for sure whether Job really lived. But there is no doubt as far as the rest of the Bible writers are concerned. He is mentioned in several books. We can read about him in Ezekiel in the Old Testament and in James in the New Testament. And the geographers aren't much more help than the historians. No one knows where the land of Uz was on the ancient map.

But these questions are not the important ones.

Job has no known nationality. He could be anyone. You might live next door to him or sit next to him on the train. In a way this helps, because Job becomes a man for all seasons and for all times.

The writer was obviously an intelligent person. He knew a lot about geography and nature. He had a wide experience of life and knew how to plan his book. He put over his points in different ways. He used both poetry and prose. He was out to capture people's imagination and he really succeeded. After all, people still read and enjoy Job today.

Could any man suffer as much as this man did? It seems too far-fetched. Yet his suffering serves a purpose. When we look at the life of a very famous man we learn something. So when we read about great suffering we can find out a lot about life. If a story is vivid enough we will probably remember it. And Job is certainly that!

1. So you think you've got problems?

Job was the man who had everything. Money, property – you name it, he had it. It was agony buying birthday presents for him. He didn't need anything. He was a wealthy farmer with a fantastic stock. **He owned 7000 sheep, 3000 camels, 1000 head of cattle, and 500 donkeys (1:3).** This made him the Number One business tycoon in the East. Of course, he was also a big employer. He had lots of animals and he needed land for them to graze on and servants to look after them. Fortunately he had plenty of both. He was the Paul Getty of those days. No one was better off than Job.

Here was a man who had really made it! And Job was not just a successful business man. His family life was booming too. In his day, a big family was an investment. Children would look after you in your old age. Many of them died young, so the more you had, the safer the future was. Life was different then. Families stuck together and children respected their parents. There was no old-age pension or social security, so if you had no children, you starved. Job was in no danger of that! **He had seven sons and three daughters (1:2).** Seven sons meant plenty of boys who would keep the family business going and build up the empire. They would carry on the family name. And three daughters was just the right number too. Any more girls would have caused problems because weddings cost money and it was the bride's father who had to dip his hand in his pocket. Still, girls tend to look after their old dad better than boys. So Job had nothing to worry about, with three healthy daughters round the house.

Job was lucky with his family life. His children really were a happy bunch. They all got on well together. In fact they enjoyed each other's company very much, and they had plenty of time to enjoy it. After all, their father was rich! They did not have to work for a living. They could get together as often as they liked and have parties. **Job's sons used to take it in turns to give a feast, to which all the others would come, and they always invited their three sisters to join them (1:4).** They took it in turns to have the family in for a slap-up meal. No one stayed away in the sulks. Everyone was invited to every party, and they all came.

It all sounds too good to be true! Job was fortunate in business. He had a successful and happy family life as well. How lucky can you get? But even that was not all. There was something more important still. Job was a religious man. He **worshipped God and was faithful to him. He was a good man, careful not to do anything evil (1:1).**

How well Job would have fitted into church life today! There are still a few people like him. They go to church twice on Sunday and to all the weekly meetings. They give out the hymn books, take the collection and almost live in church. But it's not all outward show. Their religion really matters. It makes

Job's sons used to take it in turns to give a feast.

a difference to them. Job was just like that. His faith affected every part of his life. People couldn't help noticing it. His friends were impressed and even God could say, 'Did you notice my servant, Job? There is no one on earth as faithful and good as he is' (1:8). You'd never find Job involved in anything shady. He was straight. He was as honest as the day is long, and only did what was right. In fact he was as near perfect as possible.

Now some 'good' people are not very pleasant to know. They set themselves up on pedestals, and keep everyone else at arm's length. If you dare to speak to them, they make you feel smaller than a worm. But Job was not like that. He gave advice to anyone who wanted it. If someone needed money, Job was the first to help. He would often put his hand in his pocket and dig deep each time. If anyone was in trouble he would come and lend a hand. And when people felt miserable, lonely or depressed, they sent for Job. He always knew what to say and how to help. His religion made a difference to the way he lived. He was concerned for people.

Let's move a little further into his story. Job was a good father. He really loved his children. When they enjoyed themselves he was happy. He would go to their parties and join in the fun. But he was getting old and old folks like their beds early. Job was no exception. He would put in an appearance and then go, probably when the noisy music started. But he did not forget his children once the door closed behind him. He cared about what happened to them after he left. He knew the pitfalls of parties. Youngsters can get carried away so easily. Of course, he trusted his children but just suppose . . . So the morning after the night before, **Job would get up early and offer sacrifices for each of his children in order to purify them. He always did this because he thought they might have sinned by insulting God unintentionally (1:5).** They were good children but even good people sometimes make mistakes. Job had

12

to be sure. His prayers covered all possibilities. He loved God and wanted the whole family to be right with him.

So there we are. Job was the man who had everything. His life was an example to all. He'd reached the top of the tree. He was in the prime of life and had everything any man could ask for or need. Job was safe and secure.

Except he wasn't.

That day began like any other. **One day when Job's children were having a feast at the home of their eldest brother . . . (1:13).** Everyone was out at work except the children. They were having a party. Even Job was out in the fields inspecting his farm and admiring the crops. God was in his heaven and all was well with the world.

Then tragedy struck. Murder and theft were the first blows. **A messenger came running to Job. 'We were ploughing the fields with the oxen,' he said, 'and the donkeys were in a nearby pasture. Suddenly the Sabeans attacked and stole them all. They killed every one of your servants except me. I am the only one who escaped to tell you' (1:14,15).**

Before Job could catch his breath, the nightmare got worse.

Even the weather was against him! **Another servant came and said, 'Lightning struck the sheep and the shepherds and killed them all. I am the only one who escaped to tell you' (1:16).** The sheep and the shepherds burned to a frazzle? Job couldn't believe it. Surely he would wake up soon. This must be a bad dream.

No chance! Messenger after messenger came. Each piece of news was worse than the last. Yet another servant ran up, out of breath. **'Three bands of Chaldean raiders attacked us, took away the camels, and killed all your servants except me' (1:17).**

If an amateur boxer fought the professional world champion, it would not be much of a contest. The challenger would soon be on the ropes and punches would rain on him. He would be battered to the ground. There would be nothing he could do. Job was just like that. He felt helpless. He was down for the count. Everything had been wiped out at a stroke.

Except it was not quite everything.

People get over business collapse and bankruptcy, but there are more important things in life. When trouble comes, you need the family around you. Job had lost his men and his animals but at least he had his children. He could still fall back on them. But then with a sinking heart he saw yet another messenger on his way. **'Your children were having a feast at the home of your eldest son, when a storm swept in from the desert. It blew the house down and killed them all' (1:18,19).**

This final piece of news was the knock-out punch. The fight was over. Here was suffering to end all suffering. Job was finished.

The whole story seems incredible. Could it really have happened? Life can be stranger than fiction and far more terrible. Just stop for a moment and think how you would react yourself. It would be bad enough to lose your livelihood and become bankrupt. If that happened, you might just be able to cope. But if you lost your family too, you would really be alone. Suppose they were killed in a car crash and it was their fault! As well as the grief, you would have big bills to pay. It would not be easy to pick yourself up off the floor and start again.

How did Job react to this mountain of trouble? He was a typical Oriental. He went through all the traditional Eastern customs of mourning. **Then Job stood up and tore his clothes in grief. He shaved his head and threw himself face downwards on the ground (1:20).** It seems a bit extreme to us, but it was the usual thing to do. It was just like wearing a black tie or dark clothes at a funeral today. Job got down in the dust, from which man came and to which man must return.

His mind was as torn as his shirt. It's funny how trouble makes people think. Job thought to himself, **I was born with nothing, and I will die with nothing (1:21).** We do not bring anything into the world and we do not take anything with us when we die. All the money in the world will not help when our time comes. A tax free bank balance in Switzerland does not make any difference when you are lying in a wooden box! It's only common sense really. We are born naked and we die naked. We cannot take anything with us when we go.

So Job was in the doldrums. But his next words open up an unexpected chink of light. **The Lord gave,** and now he has taken away. May his name be praised! (1:21). Was the sudden strain all too much for him? Had his mind cracked? After all, he had lost everything that mattered. It was hardly a time for singing hymns of praise!

People act strangely when death comes. Some try to get into the grave with the coffin. Others talk to the dead person and even hammer on the coffin lid. They simply can't let go. It breaks your heart. Job seemed to be behaving this way. He had nothing left yet he talked about a *God who gave*. He was obviously numb with pain! He was like many old, lonely people when they lose their family and friends. He could not admit what he had lost. He talked about the good old days. It is so much easier to live in the past when trouble comes.

But there was method in Job's madness. He looked back to the time when he had everything. It had been such a short while ago. And as he looked back, he thought about God. It was God who had given him all his animals, servants, land, prosperity and family in the first place, wasn't it? Job didn't own all these things, God did. God had loaned them to Job to look after and to use. So surely God had every right to do what he liked with what was his. If you rent a house, it does not become yours just because you live in it. You can spend a fortune on improvements. You can decorate it, inside and out. You may even begin to think it *is* yours but it isn't and never will be. It belongs to the landlord and he can do whatever he likes to it. After all he owns it.

Job recognized that God had owner's rights. The

16

Lord had given so he could take away. But the loss was still hard to bear! The pain and the separation still hurt. Job was no false optimist. He didn't just bury his head in the sand and pretend life was wonderful when it wasn't. And the agony certainly was real.

But was he being fair to God? After all, it was the Sabeans, the Chaldeans, the lightning, and the storm that had wiped out his property and family. It was a terrible run of bad luck but it was hardly God's fault, was it?

As far as Job was concerned, things like this didn't happen by chance. God had done it all because he had allowed it. God was in control of everything that happened and all was safe in his hands. That was what Job believed. So even in the depths of despair, he could lift up his head and say, **'His name be praised!'** (1:21).

Here then is something vital that we must not miss in Job's story. He was no fair weather religious man. He didn't trust God only when things were going well. He trusted him when the going got tough too. If his religion was good enough for prosperity, it was good enough for trouble. Job knew that all of his life, good and bad, was in God's hands. If God really was God, then he could do whatever he liked. In the past he had wanted to make Job rich, and now it seemed he wanted to take all that wealth away. It was God's privilege as far as Job was concerned. You see, Job believed that God had a plan for him. All the terrible things were happening for a purpose. God would work everything out for the best. Job did not know how or when, but he firmly believed that God would do it.

When illness comes to some people, they blame God. They never bother about him when everything in the garden is fine. But if they fall sick or lose a relative God gets all the blame. Why did he let it happen? Why doesn't he do something about it?

Job did not think that way. **In spite of everything that had happened, Job did not sin by blaming God (1:22).** He never even thought of complaining against him. When trouble came, Job's first reaction was to worship God, not blame him. He thanked the Lord for all he'd done for him in the past. Then he trusted him for the future. God was in charge. And that was good enough for Job.

How remarkable! Here was a man who was completely in the dark. He did not understand what was happening to him and he did not know why it was happening. Later, we will be taken behind the scenes, where the action really is. We will be able to see what is actually going on and why. But Job was not in on the secret at all. He could only see the bit that hurt. And what he saw made nonsense! Yet still he trusted God. He managed to cope with his grief and sorrow and still keep his faith. Trouble had come and, presumably, trouble would go. One thing was certain, things could not get worse.

Except that they could!

They not only could: they did. So far, Job had not been affected physically. Now he fell ill. It began with a rash. The spots spread. They became boils. From tip to toe Job was an oozing mass of pus and pain. He had some kind of leprosy. It was catching and people were afraid of it, so Job went into quarantine. The isolation ward in those days was the local rubbish dump. **Job went and sat by the rubbish heap and took a piece of broken pottery to scrape his sores (2:8).**

It must have been hard to recognize him. Once he had been a prosperous business man. Now he was a piece of filth surrounded by filth. There he sat among the broken pots and rotting food. The stench was terrible. No one dared to get too near. But even from a distance you could see him scratch. His boils itched terribly. And he didn't just tear at them with his nails. He attacked them with a jagged piece of pottery. He dragged it viciously up and down his body. He had to kill the awful itch somehow, even if it meant more pain. Scraping didn't help much, but at least it passed the time.

There was no fancy medicine or even a national health and welfare scheme for Job. Before, he had lost a great deal but at least he had still kept his health. Now he didn't even have that. Illness had struck a final blow. His cup of sorrows was full and running over.

But there was still one more drop of sorrow to come.

Job still had his wife. The little woman in his life had been spared through all the disasters. She ought to have been the best person to comfort him now. She was certainly the only one left who could help

19

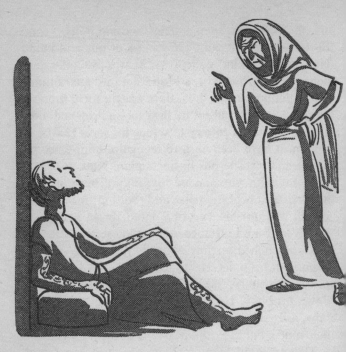

*A knife in the ribs would have been less painful than her
sharp taunts.*

him. But she was a tartar. And she knew how to nag.
She was such an expert in nagging that she could
have given lessons in it. And as for her sarcasm – it
had to be heard to be believed. She could kick a man
where it hurt most. She even seemed to enjoy it, in
spite of her husband's desperate state. 'Your
religion really helps you, doesn't it? **You are still as
faithful as ever, aren't you?**' she scoffed. 'Why don't

you curse God and die?' (2:9). Her advice to Job was simple and direct. 'Death for you, my lad, and the quicker the better!'

So Job still had his wife. But what use was she? She only made matters worse. Her cruel tongue increased his sorrow. Hard words from loved ones hurt more than anything else. A knife in the ribs would have been less painful to Job than her sharp taunts. He could have coped with anything else at that moment, even her death. After all, dead wives don't nag!

Yet Job was still in control of himself. He could still think straight, and he wasn't standing for this sort of talk, even from his wife. **'You are talking nonsense!'** he told her sharply. **'When God sends us something good, we welcome it. How can we complain when he sends us trouble?' (2:10).**

Job had some hard things to say about life, but he never lost his faith. **In spite of everything he suffered, Job said nothing against God (2:10)** He still loved and trusted God, even if faith did not bring prosperity and security. He loved God, not for what he could get out of the relationship, but simply because he loved him.

* * *

Why do the innocent suffer? They do no one any harm. Why do good people get hurt? They deserve only the very best. Why did Job have such sorrow? Even God said he was a good man.

As yet, the Book of Job offers no answer to these

questions. But already one important truth has come across, loud and clear. *God is in charge at all times.*

Some people try to turn God on and off like a tap. When life is good they ignore him. They turn him off. But as soon as trouble comes and they need an urgent answer to their prayers, they rush to turn the God tap on again. What a cheek! And what nonsense! God can do wonderful things but he is much more than Superman. He rules in all parts of our life. If we believe in him, we must see him in the good times as well as the bad and the bad as well as the good. That's one of the big lessons of the Job story. But it is not the only one. There's plenty more to come. Keep reading.

2. Testing time

Let's turn the clock back and change the scene. Before any of those terrible things happened to Job, there was plenty going on in heaven. Job knew nothing of that of course! But we are allowed to be flies on the wall and listen in to two conversations between God and Satan. The first took place before the awful events we read about in Chapter One.

SCENE I – HEAVEN
          ACTORS – GOD, SATAN (1:6–12)

GOD: Welcome, everyone. Make yourselves comfortable. These weekly reports are a good chance for us all to hear the news. Well, Satan, speak up. **What have you been doing?** Where have you been? Who have you seen? Do tell us.

SATAN: Well, God, you know me. **I've been walking here and there, roaming round the earth.** Life's much the same as usual. Nothing special to report.

GOD: And you have nothing to say? You do not live up to your name, Accuser! You are usually the first to pick holes in people. I wish you were half so keen to give credit where credit is due. But who did you see? **Did you notice my servant Job?** Look out for him. He is a faithful and good man. No one on earth can match him. Yes, you may well shrug! Job is sincere. He is a good man. He worships me and his religion is not just show. It really works. He never gets involved in shady deals. He steers clear of anything bad.

SATAN: So you say. It pays him to be good. **Would Job worship you if he got nothing out of it?**

GOD: Satan, there's no reason to talk like that. I know you've nothing to bring against Job. He is as pure as the driven snow.

SATAN: That's as maybe. But no wonder Job is faithful to you. It pays him! You make it worth his while, don't you? **You bless everything he does.** A bit of protection here, a few more head of cattle there. Job does all right out of it. Everything he touches turns to gold. Money makes money. Success breeds success. Job's on to a good thing and he knows it.

GOD: It isn't like that at all. Why do you always think the worst of people?

SATAN: Because I have as many reasons as there are people. Job is just the same as the rest. He knows which side his bread is buttered on. You even make sure he gets plenty of jam. I can prove it. All it needs is a little test. **Suppose you take away everything he has.** It would be a different story then.

We'd soon see the real Job! He wouldn't be your little pet any more. He wouldn't fawn around you then. You know what will happen if you allow that, God? **He will curse you to your face!**

GOD: You've said enough, Satan. You don't realize how wrong you are. You think you know Job. You don't. He's not just interested in what I give him. His love is true love. He loves me for myself. I'm happy to prove it to you. At least, I'll get Job to prove it to you.

SATAN: You daren't risk it! You'll be at his mercy. He'll let you down. Men always do. They're only interested in themselves. I tell you honestly, God, Job only loves you because it's worth his while. Take his wealth away and his love will disappear in a flash.

GOD: You are making a serious charge. You say that Job is totally selfish. You say that his love is a lie. Well, we'll see, Satan. **Everything he has is in your power.** You can do whatever you like to everything he has – family, lands, animals. All of it is yours to do with as you please. I give you the freedom to do your very worst. But you are not to lay one finger on Job's body. If your point is true, you will prove it, **but you must not hurt Job himself.**

SATAN: Fantastic! I never thought you'd let me get away with it. I'm off to show you the real Job. He's the world's Number One con man. Love God for nothing? There's no chance of that!

COMMENT ON SCENE I

So now we know Satan. That last scene shows him up clearly. He is the original hatchet man. He is always on the prowl, looking out for some poor, innocent victim and then sticking the knife in. He is clever too, in a sly kind of way. He knows how much God admires and trusts Job. So he plays the scene craftily. First, he slips in the mere pin-prick of an idea. Can God *really* depend on his pampered servant? Then comes the direct challenge, driven in like a huge chisel. **Take away everything he has – he will curse you to your face (1:11).**

Satan keeps his eyes open. He knows about people and their weaknesses. Take a silly old fool who has plenty of money. One day he falls for a pretty young girl. He gives her diamonds, furs, everything she asks for. In the end, she agrees to marry him. Then the trouble starts. Someone sows a seed of doubt in his mind. Does his wife really love him? Is she not really more in love with the presents he gives her? She wants the things money can buy – the good time, the fancy clothes, the gay social life. That's it. She does not want *him* at all! The old boy's eyes are opened. And the day of reckoning comes. This is exactly the picture that Satan is trying to draw. He tells us that Job 'loves' God on the surface. But deep

Is she not really more in love with the presents he gives her?

down he is only in the religion business because it pays well.

God's part in the action is interesting. He seems helpless. Satan doubts his judgement and God lets him. He does not answer his questions about Job. Is it because he can't? Of course not! God knows Job inside out. He needs no lie detectors to test anyone's faith. But he must show that Satan is wrong. He knows Job's love is real but no one else can be sure. Mightn't it be cupboard love? Job *could* be out for all he can get, couldn't he?

So God allows the test. He makes himself powerless. He promises to do nothing. He even puts himself at Job's mercy. After all, Job is his faithful follower . . . or is he? Job has to prove it.

CONCLUSION ON SCENE I

The Book of Job is not about suffering in itself. It uses the problem of suffering to look at selfish religion. Are people only religious for what they get out of God? Do they really love him? Aren't they just scratching God's back because he scratches theirs? Religion can seem a good investment, particularly if it is based on a bargain. That has nothing to do with real love, though. Real love does not ask for anything in return. If it does, it is not the genuine article.

So Job is going to be put to the test. Only he can prove that Satan is a liar. Only he can show that God is right. But that presents a problem! Job must never know why he is suffering. It has to be the real thing. Once he knows he is defending God and his honour, it will be no test at all. For God's sake, Job would have put up with anything and happily lost everything. It would be a privilege to suffer for God. But that would defeat the whole purpose of the exercise.

Job must not know what is happening behind the scenes. Only in that way will the world see the truth. Only in that way will God prove to Satan that man's faith need not depend on selfish gain. It is all up to Job.

SCENE II – HEAVEN
ACTORS – GOD, SATAN (2:1-6)

Notes: As soon as the curtain dropped on Scene I, Satan went to work on Job and he did a splendid job! As we have seen, Job lost everything. Of course he knew nothing of that first conversation in Heaven.

Now Satan returns to report. Job has done well so far. But Satan won't let him off the hook.

GOD: Well, Satan, let's hear your report this week. I'm sure you have some news for us all.

SATAN: Nothing special to report. **I have been walking here and there, roaming round the earth.** I like to do my job properly. I always report anything nasty those humans get up to. You can count on me.

GOD: What about Job? Don't tell me you didn't notice him this time! You remember Job – the faithful, clean-living fellow? The one who **worships me and is careful not to do anything evil?**

SATAN: The name does ring a bell.

I have been walking here and there.

GOD: You suggested that Job was really selfish. I know that the opposite is true. But **you persuaded me to let you attack him for no reason at all.** I agreed that he should be kept in the dark about the whole thing. You said that Job was only religious because it paid him to be. You said that a little suffering would change things. So we put him to the test. Tell us what you did to him.

SATAN: Nothing much. A little demolition work on the farm and family.

GOD: It was utter destruction! It was awful. But tell me, how did my servant Job react? What did he say when he lost everything he had?

SATAN: He took it much better than I expected.

GOD: He took it like the saint he is. You said he'd spit in my face, but he didn't. He knew that I was in control. Poor old Satan didn't even get the credit for what he'd done! The situation was never out of my hands, and Job knew it. The whole thing was fair. He still knows nothing about the test. Yet he passed with flying colours. I call that game, set and match to Job.

SATAN: Before we give out the prizes, I think I ought to tell you that the little experiment wasn't quite fair.

GOD: Not quite fair? I let you do exactly what you wanted!

SATAN: That's not quite true, if I may say so. You did attach one condition. A crucial condition as far as I'm concerned. Job himself was not to be touched. But we all know that **a man will give up everything in order to stay alive.** Everybody has his price. The torture chamber proves that. A prisoner may refuse to reveal his sources of information when he is questioned. But give him five minutes with a friendly torturer and he will sing like a canary! Activity is a bit restricted if every bone in your body is broken. Life is what matters most to people. When the chips are down, self-preservation comes out top. Nothing works like pain.

GOD: You twist the truth into lies. But what has this to do with Job?

SATAN: A great deal, Merciful One. If Job were given a good dose of pain, then he would soon change his tune. **Suppose you hurt his body – he will curse you to your face!**

GOD: One day, Satan, your cleverness will destroy you. You don't really understand Job. In fact, you don't understand mankind. People can love without self interest. Job is only one of many. You may put him on the rack. You may torture him. His body can be the battlefield. But, remember, I am God. I control events. The only power you have is the power I allow you. I make the rules and I set the limits. You can do what you like to Job. **He is in your power, but you are not to kill him.**

SATAN: Thank you. I won't need to bother you again. Job is no problem now. We'll soon see how much he loves himself. He does not love you at all! He is typical of all mankind. Men are a totally selfish lot. Even you can't do anything to change that.

COMMENT ON SCENE II

Satan doesn't give up easily! He always tries to the bitter end. But God is not afraid of the worst Satan can do. He allows him some power but he does not give him a totally free hand. He never lets the situation or Satan get out of his own control.

And as usual, events proved God right. When Satan attacked Job's body, Job did not surrender. The pain and suffering did not make him curse God. Not even his wife could do that!

So Job passed the test. **In spite of everything he suffered, Job said nothing against God (2:10).**

But the story does not end there. Job still knew nothing at all about the heavenly test. He did not know *why* he had suffered. Heaven is heaven and earth is earth. So the rest of the Book of Job brings us back down to ground level. We read nothing more about these heavenly scenes. The writer of Job wants us to know the whole story. But he goes on with the rest of the book as if nothing had happened in heaven at all. Job and his friends had no idea what God was up to. Now we are shown how they reacted to the situation as ordinary human beings. Their 'solutions' begin and end simply from man's way of looking at things. Job was an innocent sufferer. What answers could he produce for himself with a little help from his friends? We shall see in the next chapter.

CONCLUSIONS ON SCENES I AND II

There is more to life than being wealthy and healthy. That is the message so far. All is not lost if the summer holiday plans fall through. The things that happen to us here and now don't just depend on ourselves and what we think the world is all about. If faith means anything, it means believing that Someone is in charge of the world and of us. He made everything, including us, and he is working everything out according to his plan. He knows where the world is going and, in the end, he is in full control.

If we could look at life through God's eyes, we would see things very differently. In fact, we would live completely different lives. We would know not only *what* was really happening, but *why* it was happening. As it is, we don't know and we can't find out. We are just like Job. Things happen to us which shatter our little world and we can't do anything about it. Sometimes that can make us feel everything is out of control. We seem to have come from nowhere and to be going nowhere fast.

The Book of Job denies that. It shows God in control, not only of the heavens and the earth, but also of what happens to men. God is working his purpose out, even if we can't see him doing it. What is amazing is that he is on our side! He is not against

He isn't interested in treating men like puppets.

man. He's for him. God believes in man so much that, in a sense, he puts himself at our mercy. He could give us so many good things that we'd be glad to do whatever he wanted. He could even force us to believe in him and obey him.

He could, but he doesn't. He isn't interested in treating men like puppets. God does not pull the strings and make men jump to it. God allows man to be man. This means we are free to love him or not, to respond to him or to choose to ignore him altogether. We don't understand everything and we never will. But we do know enough to be free to respond to him freely in faith, with no threat of blackmail. God is not interested in buying our love. Unless it is freely given for his own sake, it is not really love at all.

It's a big encouragement to know that God is in control and that he sets limits to the power of evil. Just imagine how much evil there would be if God had set no limits. But why does he allow evil anyway? Well, if he wiped it out totally he would force us to do good and to be good. We would have no choice. We would be mere robots. God's world is more open than that! There exists good and its opposite, evil. And if we have freedom to reject God and his goodness, we must be free to accept Satan and all he stands for too.

It is bad enough to watch those who choose evil suffer the consequences, but at least it's fair. It is far worse to see those who choose good suffering evil without any apparent reason. And this brings us back to Job and his troubles. We are not up in heaven seeing things from God's point of view, but firmly stuck here on the earth. We are still left, as Job was, with the problem of why innocent people suffer. What can we say?

3. With friends like these, who needs enemies?

It is down to earth again. The scenes in heaven are left behind. The writer takes us back to Job and his problems. He is still on the rubbish dump. Things have not changed. They have certainly not got better.

Trouble shows you who your real friends are. If you do hit a sticky patch, true friends rally round. They pick you up off the floor. They help you get on your feet again. Job was a lucky man. In his trouble, his friends rushed round. They were sorry for him and came to say so. Bad news travels fast. The news of Job's tragedy spread like wildfire. His friends came to bring their sympathy. What a shock they got! It was much worse than they expected. They did not even recognize him. Job was a changed man. When they looked at him, their hearts broke. He had aged overnight. He was a broken-down old man. They were upset by the whole thing. So they joined him right there on the rubbish dump. There they sat. Their clothes were torn in sympathy. They had dust and ashes all over them. They cried their eyes out. You could hear the sighing and moaning a mile away. But what was there to say?

Hospitals make some people feel like that. It is worse if you know the patient and he is really ill. You make the effort. You go to see him. You hand over the grapes and the card. You ask how he is. Then the struggle starts. You have to keep the conversation going. You can hardly leave the minute you've arrived. Yet the patient is in no condition to speak. So what do you do? You sit there and say nothing. You feel a fool. You wish you hadn't come.

Things must have been very bad. Job's friends had nothing to say. **They sat there on the ground with him for seven days and nights without saying a word, because they saw how much he was suffering (2:13).** Some situations are as bad as that. The best thing you can do is to keep quiet.

But time is a great healer. Perhaps Job's friends hoped they would see some improvement after a week. After all, Job had done so well in the first test. He had taken the loss of his wealth and his family so bravely. But he had bottled up his feelings too long. Somehow he had to get them off his chest. So his friends got the brunt of his anger. He poured it all out! 'God **put a curse on the day I was born; put a curse on the night when I was conceived (3:2-3). I wish I had died in my mother's womb or died the moment I was born'** (3:11). Job had had enough! **'Everything I fear and dread comes true. I have no peace, no rest, and my troubles never end'** (3:25-6). He had been through such a lot. He had lost everything. No amount of pills could deaden those memories. He would have been better off dead.

Job's silent suffering had stopped his friends' mouths like a gag. But his words had the opposite effect. His violent outburst made them sit up and

38

speak up. Grief is grief, but this was going a bit too far! Job obviously needed his friends' help badly. He had to be made to see reason. There *was* an answer to his problem. How lucky he was to have friends like them! All of them thought they held the key to Job's suffering. Their solutions were not all the same, but they were variations on the one theme. Each one had three turns. One bite at the cherry wasn't good enough. Job was completely swamped with well-meant advice.

ANSWER MY QUESTION *

The next part of the story sounds exactly like a panel game. You have your team of experts. Someone asks a question and the panel members offer their answers. It went something like this.

PRESENTER : Good evening, ladies and gentlemen. Welcome to *Answer My Question*. We've another team of experts and another set of problems for you. And tonight we have a real teaser for the team. Our questioner is well known. His story is, too. It's Job, the man who had everything.

But before we meet Job and his problem, let me introduce the panel to you. Their names may not be too familiar. On my right, we have *Eliphaz* and *Bildad* and, on my left, *Zophar*. They are typical experts.

The next part of the story sounds exactly like a panel game.

Take *Eliphaz*. He's the oldest. He's a university man and he has had a remarkable experience. I'm sure he'll tell us all about it tonight. He's had a vision which has changed his whole life. If you like dreams and mysteries, then Eliphaz is the man for you.

Next we have *Bildad*. He is the

voice from the past. He's an expert in tradition. If it was good enough for our fathers, it is good enough for Bildad. He'll tell you the way things have always been done.

Last but by no means least, we have the plain man to end all plain men, *Zophar*. He always calls a spade a spade. He'll stand for no nonsense. Common sense is his speciality!

Well that's enough from me. Let's go over to our main problem of the evening. It's posed by Job.

JOB: Just look at me. **I have no peace, no rest, and my troubles never end (3:26).** What have I done to deserve this? **Why let men go on living in misery? (3:20).**

PRESENTER: Thank you, Job. I'm sure we understand the point. Well, panel, why is Job suffering?

ELIPHAZ: It's usual for the oldest to go first. So I shall. In fact, **I can't keep quiet any longer (4:1).** I've known Job a long time. He's been worth knowing, too. He's a good man. Job, **you have taught many people and given strength to feeble hands. When someone stumbled, weak and tired, your words encouraged him to stand (4:3–4).** But look at you. **Now it's** your turn to be in trouble, and you are too stunned to face it (4:5).

Let me ask you a question. Name a single case where a righteous man met with disaster (4:7). You can't! There isn't one. The good always win and the bad always lose. You reap what you sow. There's no getting away from it.

I remember once a message came . . . Like a nightmare it disturbed my sleep . . . I could see something standing there; I stared, but couldn't tell what it was. Then I heard a voice out of the silence (4:12,13,16).

I know you are all dying to know what the voice said. It went like this. 'Can anyone be righteous in the sight of God or be pure before his Creator?' (4:17).

The answer is as plain as the nose on my face. No one can. Nobody is pure compared with God. No one is good except God. In my opinion, there is only one reason for suffering. Man brings trouble on himself, as surely as sparks fly up from a fire (5:7). When trouble comes, there is only one thing to do. If I were you, I would turn to God and present my case to him (5:8).

I can prove my point. Look at the

wicked. They're all the same. **I have seen fools who looked secure,** but their prosperity is short-lived (5:3). Whenever they think themselves safe, disasters strike. They live in fear and they get what they deserve. Punishment and exile come their way. What a life! Fear hounds them all the time. And in the end, they and their children are wiped out without trace. **Like a storm, God destroys them in his anger (4:9).** You don't have to take my word for this. Ask any wise man. He'll tell you the same.

You're no exception, Job. I'm sorry, but it must be true. You're in trouble **because you have sinned so much,** and **because of all the evil you do (22:5).** It's no wonder you're in such a mess. You must have been leading a double life. You got yourself a big reputation as a do-gooder but I can guess what you got up to on the quiet. **You used your power and your position to take over the whole land. You not only refused to help widows, but you also robbed and ill-treated orphans (22:8,9).** You can't be expected to get away with that kind of thing for ever!

The cure is simple. **Make peace with God . . . and put an end to all the**

evil that is done in your house (22:21,23). Put things right with God. If you do, he will forgive you. God bandages the wounds he makes: his hand hurts you, and his hand heals.

PRESENTER: Thank you, Eliphaz, for that useful advice. Let's hope the rest of the team can keep up the good work. Who's next?

BILDAD: Eliphaz is right. **God never twists justice.** He always gives you what you deserve. History teaches us nothing else. Even **your children must have sinned against God,** Job, **and so he punished them as they deserved (8:3,4).**

They knew their stuff in the old days. **Let the ancient wise men teach you (8:10).** When people ignore God, they are skating on thin ice. Crack! The ice gives way, and they disappear without trace. They are like idiots who try to cross ravines on spiders' webs. **If they lean on a web, will it hold them up? If they grab for a thread, will it help them stand? (8:15)**

The trouble with you, Job, is simple. You just don't listen! We are not fools. We're giving you good advice. But you always know better! At least you think you do. You expect the world to fit in with your wishes. You want things to go the

44

When people ignore God, they are skating on thin ice.

way you would like. Do you think the laws of nature should be changed for *your* benefit? **Will God move mountains to satisfy you? (18:4).** What kind of a world would that be?

You need to remember what happens to the wicked. It's like being in the dark all the time. You can't see anything. You fall over things. You get caught in the traps which are set for you. You never know when something will hurt you. Disasters are always round the corner, waiting their chance. Illness, poverty and hardship come your way. It's downhill all the way to the burning fires! You can't get away from the smell of hell, when you are

45

**dragged off to face King Death!
(18:14).**

In the end, you're on your own.
There's no one left to remember you,
no one to say how good you were.
Nobody will cry at your funeral.
When your name is mentioned, folk
will shiver and look the other way
(18:20).

All this could happen to you, Job.
But you have time to change. Look
up! Turn your eyes away from yourself and from this world. Look to
God. He is the all-powerful one. **All
must stand in awe of him (25:1–2).**
You can't compare God and men.
**What is man worth in God's eyes?
(25:6).** Nothing at all! He's in-
significant. God is the one who
matters. Everything is under his
control. Life and death, air and sea,
day and night are all in his hands.
And **these are only hints of his power,
only the whispers that we have heard.
Who can know how truly great God
is? (26:14).**

So turn to him, Job. Admit you've
done wrong. Be forgiven, and all will
be well.

PRESENTER: That was straight from the shoulder!
Thank you, Bildad. I know Zophar
will be the same. He doesn't pull his

punches. Have you anything to add, Zophar?

ZOPHAR: This wise stuff is all very well. But I'm a simple man. I know **there are things too deep for human knowledge (11:6).** As far as I'm concerned, you're getting off lightly, Job. **God is punishing you less than you deserve (11:6).** You act as if you know better than the Almighty. The cheek of it! **The sky is no limit for God, but it lies beyond your reach. God knows the world of the dead, but you do not know it . . . If God arrests you and brings you to trial, who is there to stop him? (11:8,10).** No one else can help you, Job. Get down on your knees. **Put your heart right, Job. Reach out to God. Put away evil and wrong from your home (11:13,14).**

If only people would admit when they've gone wrong! What a difference it would make to *you*, Job. If only you can do that, **all your troubles will fade from your memory . . . Your life will be brighter than sunshine at noon . . . You will live secure and full of hope (11:16–18).** Turn to God for some sunshine! The minute you admit your faults, life will return to normal. But if you refuse . . .

Everyone knows what happens to the wicked. **Their one hope is that death will come (11:20).**

Of course, they start off all right. They are happy for a while. They even appear successful. But it never lasts. The higher up a person goes, the further he falls. God gets even with evil in the end! Some try to swallow their wealth. Rich living and good food swell their bellies. They want to keep it that way but they can't! **The wicked man vomits up the wealth he stole; God takes it back, even out of his stomach (20:15).**

God waits till a man gets to the peak of his career, then he swats him like a fly. All that is left is a smear on the wall.

It's your choice, Job. But watch out!

PRESENTER: It isn't often that the members of the panel are unanimous in their opinions. But we are delighted to have such clear and united advice. I'm sure Job and all of our audience would like me to thank the team for their . . .

ELIHU: What a load of rubbish! You must all excuse me, ladies and gentlemen. I thought I could keep quiet. I hoped to learn a thing or two. I was wrong. No one has answered Job. They all have good brains, but if this is the best they can do they don't deserve their fees. (He turns to the other members of the panel.) Only a fool would use your arguments. They are hopeless! Job has accused God of being unfair. And you haven't begun to answer the charge. I've got a different solution and if I don't get it off my chest, I'll burst.

PRESENTER: We didn't expect this interruption, but we always welcome the views of our audience.

ELIHU: Thank you! Listen, Job, and listen well. I'll tell you exactly what I think. See if you can answer me or not. No cheating – just man to man talk. **This is what I heard you say: 'I am not guilty; I have done nothing wrong. I am innocent and free from sin. But God finds excuses for attacking me' (33:8–10).** You couldn't be more wrong. **God is greater than any man (33:12).** He rewards people for **what they do and treats them as they deserve (34:11).** If people listened to you, they would think God never hears a prayer! **Why do you accuse God of never answering a man's complaints? (33:13).** He answers all right, and he speaks in a hundred

Listen, Job, and listen well.

different ways. The trouble is, **no one pays attention to what he says (33:14).**

We all have to learn our lesson. How can God make us do that? He sends us to school, of course – the school of suffering. The lessons are hard. We learn through pain and sickness. Most people soon get the point. They admit that they have done wrong and God makes things right again. But he's no sadist! He does not take it out on people. He does it for their own good. **God corrects a man by sending sickness and filling his body with pain (33:19).**

Don't interrupt, Job, let me finish.

Come on, you three, what do you think? Be honest! Don't let friendship hold you back. **Have you ever seen anyone like this man Job? (34:7).** He has no respect for God. He keeps bad company. **He even says that it never does any good to try to follow God's will (34:9).** Now I ask you, can that be right? **Will Almighty God do what is wrong? (34:10)** Never! He treats people exactly as they deserve. We all depend on him. He keeps us alive. If he went on strike we'd all die in a minute.

Nobody can point the finger at God as Job has done. God is in charge of everything and everybody. He is the best one to be in charge, too. Who else knows everything? Who else is all-powerful? Only God. We couldn't even complain if God went off and left us. **If God decided to do nothing at all, no one could criticize him (34:29).** He is able to do whatever he likes. That's what it means to be God. So let God be God!

Job, have you confessed your sins to God? (34:31). Have you told him you're sorry and you won't behave badly again? **Have you asked God to show you your faults? (34:32)** Give up the life you've been leading.

You're no good! We have heard you talk and we can see you're rotten through and through. You mock God and insult him to his face. How dare you! As if your sin made any difference to him! Who do you think you are? **There is nothing God needs from you (35:7).** Job, you don't know what you are talking about.

I can't make it any plainer than this. *God is just.* He treats people exactly as they deserve. He's totally fair to good and bad alike. *But he is also loving.* When he has to punish people, he is warning them to turn away from evil. If they'll only obey him, everything will be all right. God uses suffering to open people's eyes. Can't you see he's teaching you a lesson? And **he is the greatest teacher of all. No one can tell God what to do (36:22,23).**

God is in control of the heavens and the earth. Just look at the storm clouds, and feel his power and majesty! He controls the weather and the animals and everything in the world. Yet *you* think you know better than he does! That's a sure recipe for disaster. Fear God, Job. Recognize you are in the wrong. Remember **that he ignores those who**

claim to be wise (37:24). Don't be
caught in that trap.

PRESENTER: Thank you. Ladies and gentlemen, I
must apologize for this interruption.
We'll take a short break there and
rejoin the programme in a moment.
See you then.

COMMENT

This is not quite a typical panel discussion. Yet the
panel members do resemble some people we know.
Let's take a closer look at them.

Friend number one

Eliphaz is the kind of clever old man you find in the
universities. He's luckier than most, too, because a
long time ago he had a vision and this changed
his whole life. He 'got religion'. His faith is not a
second-hand affair. He has a direct line to God.

Unfortunately, Eliphaz does tend to get carried
away with the sound of his own voice. Once he
starts to speak, you can't turn him off. Worse still,
he thinks he knows the secret of the universe. He
is just like a child who has picked up a new word.
He uses it all the time. And when he takes the
wrappers off the great secret, it's a big let down!
Put in a nutshell, it's this. *Life follows a simple rule.
If you're good, you're rewarded. If you're bad, you're
punished*. Haven't we all heard that somewhere
before?

If anyone disagreed, Eliphaz had no time for him. So when Job protested that he was innocent, Eliphaz could only reply, 'Empty words! No wise man would talk as you do or defend himself with such meaningless words' (15:1–3). As Eliphaz saw it, Job had lost control. It was quite understandable, really. Depressed people often say things they don't mean. They even become aggressive, and Eliphaz recognized the signs in Job. But you are excited and glare at us in anger (15:12). That kind of behaviour didn't help anyone! It just proved that Job had a guilty conscience. He was condemned by every word he spoke. *Innocent people don't suffer.* That's the rule, and nothing can break it. Job was suffering so he must be guilty. It was as easy as that.

Eliphaz's solution came just as easily. If Job admitted his faults and turned over a new leaf, God would stop his suffering. He would be looked after and cared for. And everyone would live happily ever afterwards.

It would be easy to dismiss Eliphaz and what he has to say. After all, we know something that he did not know. Job's suffering was no punishment for being bad. It was not meant to pull him into line and make him a better person. It was part of a great cosmic test. God himself was behind it.

Eliphaz would be right ninety times out of a hundred. Sin does tend to lead to suffering. The wicked do not usually get away with it. The number in jail proves that. But in Job's case things were not what they seemed.

This time, Eliphaz did not have all the facts.

He had some of them, but they were not enough. They did not give him the right to say everything he did. He had a firm grasp of the truth but it was not the whole truth. And that led him astray because he did not allow for exceptions. He thought there was nothing else to learn. So he closed his mind to any other way of looking at things. Nothing could make the great Eliphaz change his opinions.

His logic was not very good either. He thought like this. 'You can win a fortune, if you get eight draws on the football coupon. One day you get eight draws. Bingo! You win a fortune.' It is a lovely idea, but it depends on so many other things. Two thousand other people may have got eight draws that Saturday, so the prize has to be split two thousand and one ways and you could be left with next to nothing.

Eliphaz thought that only bad people usually meet disaster and he was right. But he was wrong when he went on to say, 'So everybody who suffers a disaster must be bad.' Life is more complicated than that. Some people are more guilty than others. Some people suffer more than others too. Eliphaz was blinded by his special experience. He thought it applied to everyone. He used his own experience as a yardstick and he measured everybody else's religious state with it. And that's where he went wrong.

He certainly had some worthwhile things to say. He had a good deal of wisdom, truth and insight to offer. But he did not have a monopoly of the truth! In the end, he had no real answer to Job's predicament. He did not really understand what was happening, because he saw only part of the picture.

It was as if he wore blinkers. They hid part of the view. He saw his own little bit of the truth very clearly indeed, but he was totally blind to the rest.

Friend number two

Bildad agreed with Eliphaz. His advice was just the same. He based it on different things, though. He relied on history books, not on dreams.

Bildad was quite sure his words would drive Job to his knees. But they didn't. Why not? It wasn't because he said anything wrong. But as far as Job was concerned he missed the point badly. In fact he had a very firm grip on the wrong end of the stick! Job knew all about God's power and justice. He didn't need Bildad to tell him about that. But he also knew he didn't deserve his suffering and loss. And Bildad couldn't help him there, because the answer wasn't in the history books.

Bildad was held in the grip of tradition. He worshipped the good old days. He would have lived in the past if he could. He was really steeped in the ancient traditional beliefs and so sure that nothing new could ever happen to anyone. In fact, he was like an old orange which has a tough skin and is dry all the way through. There was not an ounce of sympathy in him. He could tell plenty of old wives' tales, but he would never listen to anything new himself. He only heard what he wanted to hear. The rest of the time he switched off. He was very good at answering questions that no one asked. In fact, Bildad had stopped thinking for himself. He depended on the past for all his ideas. He did things in a certain way, because they had always been done that way and always would be. He lived life to a set of ancient rules and that made him cold and calculating. He was remote from real life and real people in the here and now.

When we live totally in the past, this is what happens. We get stuck in a rut. We lose the capacity to learn anything new. The past is not always right for today. Certainly it can never have the last word on today's problems. We need new understanding and new insights because there are always new problems to face. Sometimes, old ideas get in the way even when they are true and right. Job knew that God was just. He believed that one day the wicked would be paid back for all their evil deeds. But that wasn't his problem. *He'd done nothing wrong – yet he was still on the receiving end.* Why? Bildad's dusty history books couldn't give him an answer.

Friend number three

Zophar was the simple man. He was the average person, the man opposite you in the train or behind you in the queue. He oozed common sense! He knew all about everyone's problems. In his opinion, it is only the experts who complicate things. Apply a little common sense and the answers come quickly and easily enough.

Zophar would have made a good politician. If things did not fit in with his views, he simply ignored them. He talked as if his way was the only one. When he was seriously challenged, he just shouted louder and drowned out the opposition.

He seemed to take a vicious delight in gory details. His description of the fate of the wicked is very vivid! He is like an eye-witness at an accident. You ask him for the simple facts and he gives you details about bits of legs and pools of blood. He enjoys it too much. It makes you feel sick!

Everything was black and white for Zophar. There were no shades of grey in him. The wicked get their deserts, so Job has no right to complain. He should take his medicine like a man and try to live better in the future. It was no use moaning about injustice. That only clouded the issue.

Many religious people are like Zophar. They pretend that life is simple. They like things to be black and white. After all, most people do if they're honest. Life is easier that way. Too many questions make too many problems. Unfortunately, ordinary life can be very awkward. The world is complicated and so are people. Common sense solutions are not always the best. Sometimes answers only come when we take a problem and look at it from all angles. That is our only hope. We must not act like the ostrich. He sticks his head in the sand so that he can't see the danger any more. But that does not mean it has gone away. No, we should not imitate him! God has given us minds. And we must use them.

A voice from the audience

Elihu appeared from nowhere and interrupted. He waited till his elders had had their say then he burst out: 'I am young, and you are old, so I was afraid to tell you what I think. But I can't hold back the words . . . I can't stand it' (32:6,18,20).

Sometimes the young can teach the old a thing or two. Elihu was the original angry young man. He wanted to put the world to rights. And he was absolutely sure that he had God's own answer to Job's problem. **It is the spirit of Almighty God that comes to men and gives them wisdom . . . So now I want you to listen to me (32:8,10).**

We are not told how Job reacted to all this. Perhaps Elihu was nearer to helping him than any of the rest. But being near is not good enough. You can be near a football ground or a ball park on the day of a big match. You can even be at the gate. But you need to be inside to get the atmosphere.

Elihu introduced a new note. He looked at suffering in a different way. He suggested that it wasn't simply a matter of reaping what you sow. Pain isn't just punishment. It can actually be good for you! **God corrects a man by sending sickness and filling his body with pain (33:19).**

Elihu was right there. A death in the family does make people think. If you go to a funeral and look at the faces, you can see that. A spell in hospital makes the most unlikely people talk about the meaning of life. Suddenly it matters. After all, they may not have much more of it left!

So pain can be good for us. It sounds silly, but it's true. No one wants a child to burn his hand in the fire. But if he does, he won't make the same mistake again in a hurry. He has learned a useful lesson. Or take drug addiction. If you see a drug addict and watch him destroy his body and mind, you get a

Elihu's view of suffering is rather like the life story of the caterpillar.

nasty shock. No one wants to see junkies die, but if you do, you'll never want a fix yourself. It's a sharp warning.

Elihu spoke sound sense. His fine words did not solve Job's problem, but his speech did serve a purpose. It points us to the lessons we can learn through suffering. Even Job learned something, as we'll see.

Elihu's view of suffering is rather like the life story of the caterpillar. It is a little grub-like thing, crawling around all the time. It is always hungry and looking for a new leaf to eat. Then suddenly it stops. It wraps itself up in a silky ball. It makes a cocoon to cut it off from the world. And there it hangs. But then the struggle begins. The little grub shoves and shakes. It tries to burst the bag it is wrapped in. It wants to break out of the chrysalis. That takes a lot of effort and pain. It has to fight all the way. In the end, it is worth it all. The caterpillar becomes a beautiful butterfly. Without the pain and suffering, that butterfly would be a helpless cripple. As it struggles, its wings develop and become strong. Then it can fly. But was the suffering worth it?

CONCLUSION

Suppose you had asked Job that question as he struggled in his tight little cocoon of pain. His answer might well have been a tortured 'No!' But let's hear how he put it himself.

4. What did I do to deserve all this?

Dear God,
Nobody understands me. There's no one else I can turn to. So I am writing to you. I'm desperate. Please help me.

Why? Why? Why? Why this suffering? Why me? What have I ever done to deserve this kind of treatment? I wish I'd never been born, never lived. It was bad enough when my business went bust and my family were killed. I didn't complain then. I didn't even complain when I got the disease. I was faithful to you, but it hasn't done me much good. I could just about take it on my own. But then that terrible trio arrived. When they started to weep and wail, something cracked inside me. I couldn't keep the words back any longer. I have had to put up with so much suffering. **I am tired of living (7:16).** I would rather be dead.

Eliphaz tried to put me right. He was full of weird ideas. He brought in all his philosophy and dreams! He did not understand that my suffering is your fault, God. You **lined up** your **terrors against me,** one on top of the other. **Why won't you give me what I ask? Why won't** you **answer**

That terrible trio . . . started to weep and wail.

my prayer? (6:8) I have never gone against your will. I have never broken your commandments. **Why use me for your target practice?**

If ever I needed friends it was in this mess! I needed people who would stick by me and support me. But who turned up? A bunch of accusers! They are no better than one drop of water on a boiling hot day in the middle of the Sahara Desert. They condemn me when I have done nothing wrong.

Leave me alone, God, I beg you. My life makes no sense at all. **Won't you look away long** enough for me to swallow my spittle? Can't you ever forgive my sin? (7:19,21) And won't you take my fine friends with you when you go? I won't miss them!

Eliphaz was bad enough. But then came Bildad with his advice. He should have saved it for the agony columns. *You* know Bildad. He is full of old wives' tales. Whenever I see him coming I feel like chanting, 'Tell me the old, old story.' He said that my children were a bad lot. What a nerve! They weren't, God. You know that as well as I do. They were good to their old father. But what's the point of arguing with you? How can a man win his case against God? Should I try force? Try force on God? Should I take him to court? Who would make him go? (9:2,19)

I don't understand what you are up to. I am innocent and faithful, but my words sound guilty, and everything I say seems to condemn me (9:20). I am storm-tossed and I can't see the reason why. Are you just a destroyer? You sit up in the sky and watch me. And when terrible things happen, you just laugh. You must be a sadist. Is it right for you to be so cruel? (10:3).

I am terribly confused! Religious teachers tell us one thing, but experience tells us the opposite. They say that God only punishes the wicked. That makes me a thoroughly bad man because I am suffering so much. Yet I'm not *that* wicked! So God, who is wrong? Have the teachers made a big mistake, or am I crazy? Which is it?

I wish you were a human being, then I could take you to court. I'd look for an impartial judge. He'd try our case fairly. Are you right or am I? We need an outsider to decide between us. But you are the judge and the jury as well. **Stop punishing me, God! Keep your terrors away! (9:34)**

I am tired of living . . . **Tell me! What is the charge against me? (10:1-2)** Give me a chance. I'm innocent. Let me prove it. You can't possibly be as cruel as you seem. You made me, and now you are tearing me apart bit by bit. **Remember that you made me from clay; are you going to crush me back to dust? (10:9)**

You hunt me down like a lion . . . You always plan some new attack. Why, God, did you let me be born? I should have died before anyone saw me. Isn't my life almost over? Leave me alone! Let me enjoy the time I have left (10:16-20).

Zophar tried to help. I'll give him that. With his typical blunt blustering, he tried to ram my sins down my throat! 'Own up like a good little boy. Tell the truth and God will reward you.' Who does he think I am?

People laugh at me. I don't know why. I'm not stupid. I know that you are in control of everything, God. I don't have any argument with Eliphaz, Bildad and Zophar. *You* are my problem! I only want to state my case. Give me that chance, please!

Speak first, O God, and I will answer. Or let me speak, and you answer me. What are my sins?

**What wrongs have I done? What crimes am I
charged with? (13:22,23)** I know that you are
God and that you are great. I know that I am
asking a lot. But is it too much? **Why do you
treat me like an enemy? (13:24)** Let me prove
my innocence. Give me a chance. Any time, any
place, but give me a chance.

My friends wouldn't leave me alone. They
knew they weren't doing me any good, but that
didn't stop them. It was like those toys with
rounded bottoms. You knock them down and
they roll back up. It was like that. They
would not leave me alone. They kept bouncing
back for another Job-bashing session. **I have
heard words like that before.** I told them
straight, 'The comfort you give is only torment'
(16:1,2). But it did no good. They would not
stop.

**You have worn me out, God. I am skin and
bones . . . People sneer at me; they crowd round
me and slap my face (16:7–10).** You have no pity
for me. In fact, you treat me like a wax doll.
You stick pins in me and watch me suffer. God,
**I have cried until my face is red, and my eyes are
swollen and circled with shadows . . .(16:16).**
What good does it do? You must be made of
stone. **I want someone to plead with you for me,
as a man pleads for his friend (16:21).** Is there no
one in heaven like that? Will no one stand up
for me and take my side?

Why should I take it all lying down? I'll tell

the whole world that you are to blame, God! You have done all this terrible harm to me. **You've taken away all my wealth and destroyed my reputation (19:9).** I am all alone. My relatives and friends have gone. I'm treated like a dog. **My wife can't stand the smell of my breath, and my own brothers won't come near me (19:17).** Everybody has turned against me.

I hope somebody is writing all this down. I just hope somebody is taking notes, preferably in granite. Then they will last for ever and everyone will know what God is really like!

Please forgive me for talking like this. **I know there is someone in heaven who will come at last to my defence (19:25).** I believe that one day I will see you face to face, God. Then you'll be my friend. You won't turn me away.

I don't know what I'm saying! **When I think of what has happened to me, I am stunned, and I tremble and shake (21:6).** Why do you let the wicked get away with it, God? They tell you to leave them alone and you do what they want. **They live out their lives in peace and quietly die without suffering (21:13).** Yet look at me! I don't understand you. I just don't understand. How can I judge Almighty God? Yet the wicked get off scot-free. Everyone turns out for their funerals. No one accuses them or pays them back for all they've done.

I wish I knew where to find you. I wish I knew how to get where you are. Then I could convince you. I have worked out all my arguments. I know I'm innocent. If you would only listen, you would pronounce me 'Not guilty'. I know you are there, God, even if I can't see you, and I know you will fulfil what you have planned for me – whatever it is. I do still trust you, God, but I **will insist on my innocence to my dying day (27:5).**

I've gone on too long, God. I'm sorry, but let me say it all just one more time.

I wish life was as it used to be. Those were good days, God. You were wonderful to me then. It was lovely – the home, the children, the farm. I was in local government and everybody spoke well of me. 'Good old Job!' they used to say. I wasn't selfish either. I helped the poor and the orphans. Even if I say it myself, I was good to people.

All I expected in return was a quiet life. I looked forward to a nice, peaceful retirement and a sweet and gentle slipping away at the end. But now look at me. **Men younger than I am make fun of me now! . . . They think they are too good for me, and even come and spit in my face (30:1,10).** Why? **Because God has made me weak and helpless . . God seizes me by my collar . . . He throws me down in the mud; I am no better than dirt (30:11,18,19).** I have cried to you, God. I have begged and pleaded with you! Yet you ignore me. How cruelly you are treating me!

I am innocent. Bring out the scales of justice and weigh me and all I've done. I am not afraid! I have nothing to hide. There are no skeletons

Bring out the scales of justice and weigh me and all I've done.

in my cupboard. My life is an open book. **I swear that every word is true (31:35).**

For God's sake, is there no one there? Answer me, God Almighty. Give me an answer. Please.

Your faithful servant (and I mean it),

JOB

Job's words are moving. We would be strange people if they did not affect us. They show how agitated his state of mind was. One moment he was up and the next he was down. Sometimes he was so sure of himself, and at other times so helpless and afraid. It was only natural. Suppose *you* lost a loved one. You might behave just like Job. Your moods could change just as quickly. One moment you might be crying into your handkerchief and the next smashing the dishes in a fit of anger. You might be brave during the day and yet feel lost and alone at night. Job was like that. It wasn't so much the loss of the farm, the family, and his reputation that hurt, though these obviously did matter a great deal. Much more serious, he was losing his grip on his faith. Or to be more accurate, he had two bits of a puzzle and they did not fit together. Yet they were the only two pieces there were! They simply *had* to fit – somehow.

All that Job said was part of his struggle to fit his theory about God to his experience of real life. They just didn't go together. He believed that God punished the wicked and rewarded the good. But in his case, the opposite was happening. He was a good

man and he was being punished for it! The two bits
didn't fit.

Like his friends, Job had a fixed idea about God.
They had put him in a little box, and wanted to keep
him there. But God is bigger than all the boxes or
pigeon-holes we try to put him in! The story of Job
is a story of how boxes are broken and ideas of God
change.

We have seen how Job's God-box was smashed.
But what would replace it? So far we have no idea.
And was his traditional view of God completely
wrong? It was certainly true in part. As a rule God
does punish the bad and reward the good. But like all
rules, it does not answer every case.

Job was on the verge of something big. He often
talked to God. Even at his worst moments he did not
give this up. Sometimes he simply cried out in panic
or anger. There was nothing else to do and in a
strange way it was enough. He knew that God would
hear him. But it was like writing a letter to solve a
problem. You can sort things out so much more
quickly if you can meet the person face to face.

Did Job believe that he would meet God when he
died? He certainly did, but he wasn't sure how. He
had no guarantee that his wrongs would be righted
in the after-life. He simply did not know about it,
because he was born hundreds of years too soon.

Today we have the information that Job needed.
We know how Jesus came back from the dead and
proved that there is life afterwards. And we have his
promise that there will be rewards and punishments
on the other side of the grave. But Job had no New

Testament, and without it he had no peace about the future. God certainly gave him an answer but it was in his terms and did not depend on Job's conditions. When it came, it was far more than poor Job had bargained for!

5. A word in edgeways

Heaven, Friday

Dear Job,
  At first I thought I would write to you. Now I have a better idea. I'll come and see you myself.

GOD

If only Job had had a letter like that to prepare him, but he didn't! God simply arrived without any warning. And Job got what he wanted – or did he?

The sky grew dark. The rain pelted down. Lightning flashed across the sky. Thunder boomed loud and clear, and God spoke to Job.

'**Who are you to question my wisdom? (38:2)** Don't show your ignorance. **Stand up now like a man and answer the questions I ask you (38:3).** You claim to know so much. All right, if we are going to play at quiz games, I've got one or two questions for you.

'**Were you there when I made the world? (38:4)** Come on, tell me all about it! **Who decided how large it should be (38:5),** and who did the measuring? How is the earth supported? Who laid the foundations for the world? Who was it, Job?

'It was I, the Lord God. I control the seas and the

oceans. I control the daylight and the dawn. I tell the sun when to get up and when to go to bed. I control this world and all the worlds. I control the light and the darkness.

'Have you seen how snow and hail are made? Have you been to my weather factory? **If you command the lightning to flash, will it come to you and say, "At your service"? (38:35)** No, Job! Sun, rain, wind, sleet or snow are all at my command.

'Put your umbrella away and look up, Job. Look up at the stars! It's my power that keeps them there and moves them across the skies. **Can you guide the stars season by season and direct the Great and the Little Bear? (38:32)**

'But that's only a small part of nature, Job. Think about the animal world. Lions, ravens, goats and donkeys – you name them – I control them. I care for them all and I make them what they are. They are all so different because I have different purposes for them. You simply cannot understand. The ostrich can run like the wind, but don't ask him to fly!

'All Nature is in my hand, Job. Look at the eagle perched up there, high on the crags. Or take the horse! Man may ride him but I hold the reins. The Lord God controls them all.

'And just think of the jokes of my creation, Job. They make the mind boggle. Behemoth and Leviathan are nonsense creatures as far as man is concerned. But I made them both as I made you.

'Ah, Job, who are you? **You challenged Almighty God; will you give up now, or will you answer? (40:1–2). Are you trying to prove that I am unjust – to**

put me in the wrong and yourself in the right? (40:8)
I have to laugh. Try to be God for a day! If you could
just control mankind, I would be the first to take my
hat off to you.'

Can you believe your ears? After everything Job
has gone through, this is all God says to him. It seems
rather weak! But the words only sound so feeble to
us because we are just reading them from a book. It
was different for Job. He heard them from God's own
mouth. The living Lord spoke to him. Job actually
met God. He heard his voice and felt his presence.
He saw just a little of God's glory and power. He
only glimpsed them but they were there. For a
moment he saw creation through the eyes of the
Creator. He looked at the world, at nature, at
everything God had made; and he saw that God was
in control.

Job had asked to meet God and he got what he
wanted. But he did not get the answer he wanted or
expected! We have to be careful when we pray.
God always gives us what we ask for. But he
gives it in his own way and that may be very
different from what we expect. Job's prayer was very
daring. He wanted God to judge him, because he
was so sure that he was innocent. And in a way he
was right. There was never any question about Job's
life and goodness in God's mind. He knew that Job
was the very best. But that was not the problem.

Job's problem was his idea of God. It was a very
clear and fixed idea. He saw God as the Great

Avenger. If a man was bad, God punished him and that man suffered. But now, the simple picture lay shattered in its frame. He, Job, was a better man than most, yet he was suffering so terribly. Why? What did it all mean? God could not tell him the whole truth of course. That would have been easy but it would have made nonsense of the test. God could have said, 'Job, you are suffering because you are being tested. I want to see if you really love me.' But if he had said that, it would have been no test at all, and no one would ever have known the truth. *Is it possible to love God when he gives us nothing?* That was the big question. And secrecy was very important if the test was going to be fair.

Job had another fixed idea as well. He thought that man was the most important thing in the universe. Everything depended on man and so the world was really made for man's benefit. God had to challenge that idea too. It made him look too small. He saw the danger behind Job's questions and complaints. That was why he spoke to Job about the vastness of creation and not about the problem of suffering. Somehow Job's eyes had to be taken off himself. His blinkers had to be removed, so he could see the whole scene through God's eyes.

So God came to Job. He showed him that the world didn't revolve around man and his concerns. It was God-centred not man-centred. Man was just a creature. He must not expect to read the Creator's mind! His Maker could understand him but he would never understand his Maker. Sometimes he would be left completely in the dark when God did something.

If that happened, he shouldn't be upset or even surprised. It was only to be expected. Let God be God.

God came. He took the initiative. He came and met Job and talked to him. He wanted to help. And once Job had met God, he was a changed man. His questions had not disappeared. They were still there. But he could look at them in a different light now. God was no longer a theory or an idea. He was a living reality.

Job could not put it all into words. It's often the way! Something wonderful happens and we cannot tell anyone because words fail us. If you have ever been in love you know what it is like – but could you ever describe it to someone else? If that someone else had never been in love, he would simply not understand. Wait until he meets someone special! Then he will know for himself. A thousand text books or poems could not teach him that feeling. In the same way, Job knew he had met God. But the experience was far too big for words.

Job had been given no explanation of his sufferings. But he had gained something far more valuable instead. He had met God and listened to him. Now he found peace. He had no more complaints because he had no more fears. God had seemed far away once, but now Job knew how near he had been all the time. The Creator was totally involved in the world he had made, and totally involved with man and his needs. No matter what happened now, Job was happy. God was close. He was in charge and that was enough.

People are always asking questions about God. Does he exist? Where is he? And so the list goes on. These are not silly questions. They are serious and difficult ones. Often it is hard to answer them. The experts argue about them and discuss them endlessly. But perhaps they are going about things in the wrong way. If God is God, then he's very different from us. In a sense, he is beyond human understanding. We can only know what he tells us about himself. Once we meet him ourselves, we are sure that there are answers to our questions. They don't come all at once. Sometimes it takes a lifetime to find only a few, but we do at least begin to learn. If we know God personally, it makes such a difference. We find that we can live with our questions and problems. One day we know that we will have all the answers. And until then we should be content to wait and trust him.

6. God rules—O.K!

In the Middle Ages, a little village in Germany was protected from the plague. The villagers believed that God had saved them, and their descendants still remember the great escape. Every ten years they prepare and present a Passion play. It is the story of how God saved the world by the life and death of Jesus. It takes a long time to get the play ready for performance and people come from all over the world to see it. It lasts for over five hours. Thousands pack the auditorium for each performance. But the actors get little applause for their efforts. At the end of the last scene, there is almost total silence. Everyone files out quietly. The experience is so shattering that words fail you. It would seem like sacrilege to clap!

Even a play can have that effect. But suppose you actually saw God in action. Suppose you met him yourself, not on the stage but in real life. Job did that.

When Job met God, he knew he'd already said too much. **I will not try to say anything else. I have already said more than I should (40:4,5).** But once the first magic of the moment was over, he was able to find his tongue again. And it was a very different Job from the man who wanted to take God to court. Just listen to him!

I know, Lord, that you are all-powerful; that you can do everything you want . . . I talked about things I did not understand, about marvels too great for me to know (42:2,3).

Job saw it all now. He had built up an impressive picture of God, but it had been a wrong one. He had based all his judgements on that picture, so they were wrong too. Now he could see his mistakes. How could he dare to lay down the law to God when he was so ignorant? He had no right to question God anyway. How dare he criticize the Creator for the way he dealt with his creatures? Yes, Job's eyes were opened wide. How wrong he had been. He still had his questions, but now he was content to leave the answers in God's hands. After all, there was no safer place. God knew all about Job's sufferings. The whys and wherefores were no puzzle to him. And that was enough for Job.

What a change! Before, Job had wanted a fight with God, no holds barred. Now it was all so different! Something important had happened. It was very simple but it made a big difference. As Job himself put it, 'Then I knew only what others had told me, but now I have seen you with my own eyes' (42:5).

Have you ever met a very important person? If you have, you may have been surprised! We build up our own pictures of the people in the headlines, but in real life they often turn out to be quite different. In June 1977 the Queen of England celebrated her Silver Jubilee. She had to meet lots of important people but she also talked with many ordinary folk. They had read about her and seen her on television.

They thought they knew all about her. In their minds she was a regal, distant figure who knew nothing about their way of life. But they were wrong. How different she was when you met her! The china figure from the newspaper pictures actually stopped and spoke. She really cared about ordinary people. She was the Queen, but she was friendly too.

Job's imagination had worked overtime. He had built up a detailed picture of God. But now he had actually met him, that picture was shattered to pieces. The real God was far greater than Job had ever imagined! And that made him see himself in a different light too. That always happens when people meet God. We may think we are good when we only compare ourselves with other people. But when we look at God, we see ourselves in a new light. We are sinners! We can never match up to him. After all, he is perfect.

At last, Job realized this. No wonder he felt sorry for the things he had said! **I am ashamed of all I have said and repent in dust and ashes (42:6).**

We know exactly how he felt. It is always dangerous to talk about people, especially if you do not know them very well. Sometimes we think they are nasty and say so. Then they turn out to be very nice indeed. At once we feel really foolish and embarrassed. The same thing happens when we talk about God. We do not really understand him. We think we do because we each have our pet theories about him. But when our ideas do not fit the ups and downs of real life, we may get angry and say stupid things. There is only one answer to our problem.

81

We must meet God personally. Then we will get rid of our wrong ideas about him. But it is an uncomfortable experience. And it's hard to swallow your own bitter words.

If we do meet the living God, a relationship begins. God becomes our friend. And as time goes on, the relationship deepens. Of course, things do not fall into place all at once. We do not understand the world and all its mysteries overnight! But we do know the God who controls everything. And that helps us to cope with the surprises and problems of life.

All the best stories have a happy ending and Job's is no exception. At last God sorted things out and he left no loose ends. Satan's vandalism came to nothing in the long run.

Mind you, Job's friends got it in the neck from God! He was really angry with them. **You did not speak the truth about me, as my servant Job did (42:7).** It's obvious what God thought about the panel's opinions! They were all wrong. They had lied about God. They had not done it intentionally of course, but they were wrong all the same. It would be a long time before they could wear the label of 'expert' again. They deserved to be disgraced, to have their reputations dragged through the mud. They were foolish, unloving people and God showed them up to be so.

But he wasn't too hard on them. He gave them a let-out clause. **Now take seven bulls and seven rams**

Job's friends got it in the neck from God!

to Job and offer them as a sacrifice for yourselves
(42:8). That was a pretty steep fine, even for well-off
people, but worse was to come! Eliphaz, Bildad and
Zophar would only be forgiven if Job prayed for

them. If he did, then God promised, 'I will answer his prayer and not disgrace you as you deserve' (42:8).

What were they to do? They had let Job down. Would he do the same to them? They would be in a nasty mess if he did! But Job let bygones be bygones. He came to their rescue. They brought the animals and Job prayed for his friends. Naturally God kept his promise. Eliphaz and company were given a free pardon.

But what happened to Job himself? After he had prayed for his three friends, the Lord made him prosperous again and gave him twice as much as he had had before (42:10). When we read that, it is easy to fall into a trap. Job had suffered evil yet he bore no grudges. Now he was getting his just reward. But he was not being awarded first prize for showing mercy. If we think that, we are making a big mistake. He hadn't done anything to deserve rewards or punishments. God made him prosperous again to show that the test was over.

God was simply putting right all the evil Satan had done. Satan himself didn't dare to show his face. He was thoroughly disgraced. Things returned to normal, and Job was restored to his former position of wealthy prosperity. He still had some family left, and at last they came up trumps. All Job's brothers and sisters and former friends came to visit him and feasted with him in his house. They expressed their sympathy and comforted him for all the troubles the Lord had brought on him (42:11). And they did not come empty-handed. Each of them gave him some money and a gold ring (42:11).

Job died a happy old man. In his younger days he had been blessed by God. Now he was old, he received even more. God doubled his money. **Job owned fourteen thousand sheep, six thousand camels, two thousand head of cattle, and one thousand donkeys (42:12).** He was very rich indeed.

But he was given something even more important as well. God gave him back his family. He married again and became the proud **father of seven sons and three daughters (42:13).** The daughters were girls to remember! **There were no other women in the whole world as beautiful as Job's daughters (42:15).** The older we get, the more we like to see pretty things. How Job must have enjoyed watching his girls grow up! There's nothing like a young family to keep you young.

Job was a lucky man. He saw his children grow up, marry, and have families of their own. He even saw his grandchildren's babies. **He died at a very great age (42:17).** Job had plenty of time to think. He would sit with his grandchildren and his great-grandchildren in the long summer evenings and he would wonder. His mind would go back to his suffering by the rubbish heap. Had those terrible things really happened? It was hard to believe them now! He had certainly gone through the mill in the past. He must have often asked himself what it was all about. But even years later, there was no glimpse behind the scenes for Job. He knew nothing about any test.

Job saw his children grow up, marry and have families of their own.

He was a changed man too. He had come from the depths of despair to the heights of wealth and happiness. But there was an even bigger difference than that. Job had met God. Now he knew what God was really like. Now he saw how narrow his old ideas had been. The Lord was not a faraway figure on a Judge's bench who rewarded the good and punished the bad. He was intimately involved with the whole of his world, and especially with mankind's affairs. Job's ideas had become so much clearer since he had met his Creator. He had talked, or rather listened, to God and he had learned a lot. Now nothing could shake his faith! Even if the whole world was against him and everything went wrong, it would not matter! God was with him. Nothing could come between them. God really cared for him. And that was the important thing.

'But these are just words,' you say. 'It's just a story with a happy ending.' And so it could be. But we can come to know God today just as Job did centuries ago. And if we do, we too will find that the experience is not only worthwhile. It is worth everything.

St Paul knew exactly how Job felt when he asked, 'Who, then, can separate us from the love of Christ? Can trouble do it, or hardship or persecution or hunger or poverty or danger or death?' His answer was crystal clear. 'No, in all these things we have complete victory through him who loved us! For I am certain that nothing can separate us from his love: neither death nor life, neither angels nor other heavenly rulers or powers, neither the present nor the future, neither the world above nor the world below – there is nothing in all creation that will ever be able to separate us from the love of God which is ours through Jesus Christ our Lord' (Romans 8:35,37–9).

7. The point of it all

The story of Job says different things to different people. If you look at some of the books about it, you will see that. It is rather like a wedding. Different people go for different reasons. A husband might be interested in the food and drink while his wife only has eyes for the clothes. The marriage ceremony itself may seem unimportant to both of them. Yet that is the reason why they are there! It is like that with the Book of Job. It sets us off on some important discussions but we must make sure we do not get too far from the words of the story itself. After all, the words in the Bible are the important thing. If we stick to them we can't go too far wrong.

Job's story is written from the human angle. His suffering and pain are very real and they pose genuine questions. But the story is interesting in another way too. We are given a 'heaven's eye view' of all that happened. While Job suffered by the rubbish heap, we were allowed to eavesdrop on God and Satan. And if we put heaven and earth together, one thing becomes clear. Events are not always what they seem to be. Even when we cannot see God's hand in things, it is still there. We may be puzzled, but he is in control. And he understands his purposes, even if we do not.

Why do men and women love God? Why does

anyone believe in him or worship him? That is the very question the Book of Job asks. Sometimes we can do the right thing for the wrong reason. It is even possible to love God from bad, selfish motives. Some people are interested in religion only because they get something out of it in return. Lots of us are more like that than we dare to admit. Our faith is strong when life is comfortable, but when things go wrong we complain about God.

Selfish religion is like a bad apple. It looks nice on the surface but it is rotten at the core. Satan scoffed at all faith and worship as selfish cupboard-love. But Job proved him wrong. He passed the test with flying colours and shut up Satan's nasty accusations. He showed that religion without strings is possible. Man does not always look for rewards. He can love God for himself alone.

The test showed Satan up in his true colours too. He is still the world's champion troublemaker! He takes the worst side of human nature and plays on it. He drags men down! But his power is limited, because God is always in control. He allows Satan some freedom but keeps his own hands firmly on the reins.

Amazingly, God was being tested too. In a sense, he put himself at Job's mercy. His good name depended on Job. And it's much the same today. Things don't really change. Often God chooses to depend on human beings in this way. When we say we believe in him, we act as his advertisement. It's a big responsibility.

After all, when people search for evidence of God, they look first at the lives of his worshippers. They even judge God by how his followers behave. And they are right in a way, because if a person really believes in God, it should make a difference to his life. God is certainly powerful enough to change people. But men are strange creatures! Believers' behaviour so often lets them down, and God's good name suffers as a result.

The opposite is also true of course. If we come across a good man like Job, we really sit up and take notice! Something has made a difference to him. What is that something? Let's examine Job's relationship with God and try to find out.

Through his suffering, Job discovered God's love for him in a new way. And he found out how to love God in a new way too. The Lord of the universe is not a tyrant! He does not beat his people into submission. He is not like that at all. After all, he invented love and he knows true love must come freely. It cannot be forced if it is to keep its value. So God never *makes* people love him like puppets on a string. In Job's case, he even made love as difficult as possible. Could *you* love God if he seemed to throw you on the rubbish heap?

So Job's test was a test of love. He came through it well, but it was painful. He really suffered! Yet he still praised God. That is a powerful lesson for us. If we were suffering and in pain, could we pass the test as well as he did? Notice, by the way, that Job never praised God *for* his suffering. Instead he praised God *in* his suffering. It may sound like splitting hairs but there's an important difference. It's well worth thinking about.

But we are still faced with the problem of suffering. And it is a big problem. It causes so many difficulties. It even stops people in their tracks. They begin to believe in God, but when they meet suffering, they can get no further along the faith trail. 'God simply cannot exist,' they say. 'If he did, he would not allow people to be hurt.' So suffering puts a large question-mark over faith for many.

Pains aren't the kind of things you add up or subtract. Try to answer this. Add together my head-ache, your homesickness, the cat's sore paw and the distress caused by an earthquake. That's not a sum at all. It doesn't make any sense. No single person or thing can feel all the pain.

But that still leaves us with the problem of one particular individual's suffering. And here we come to a dead end. There's a limit to our imagination. We think that the world, nature and even God think and function in exactly the same way that we do. Do we have any real reason to suppose that? Everything cannot be made to fit in with our ideas or be judged by our standards.

The atheist and the Christian both need to produce an answer to the problem. One thinks that God is irrelevant, the other that without God there is no hope of any answer at all.

The agnostic is the only one who's really entitled to ask, 'If there is a God, why is there so much suffering in the world?' He is the man who puts 'don't know' on all the forms. He simply likes to sit on the fence, because he can never be sure. The Book of Job can be a great help to him if only he

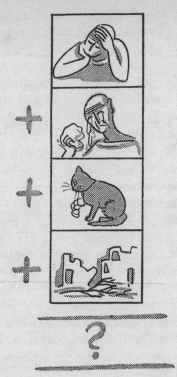

Add together my headache, your homesickness, the cat's sore paw and the distress caused by an earthquake.

will read it. It can show him how to sort out his ideas about God.

Eliphaz, Bildad, Zophar, Elihu, and even Job, had certain ideas about what God was like. They saw him as an all-powerful Judge who rewarded the good and punished the bad. They were quite right about that of course. The Bible tells us very clearly that we live in a moral universe. It is controlled by a just and fair God who does reward good and punish evil. But this does not tell us all there is to know about God, or about evil. All suffering is not caused by sin! Job's certainly wasn't. Nor is much of the suffering we see around us today. The innocent still suffer just as Job did. So when we talk about God and his justice, we have to be careful. We have our picture of him, but it is not complete.

Above all, we must not pretend that part of the truth is the whole of it. It is true, for example, that pain can bring people to their senses. God knows that, and he often uses suffering in that way. But not all pain makes all people better and stronger. This must be said again and again. Sometimes it can drive them out of their mind. God can use suffering for good. That is true but it is only part of the truth. We must be careful not to muddle a part with the whole.

For Job and his friends then, the problem of suffering highlighted their real difficulty. Their God was too small, or, at least, their vision of him was too small. They had a fixed idea about him and they clung to it obstinately. Then Job met God! The experience blew the lid off all his ideas about suffering. But it left him with clear ideas about his creator.

You would think we would know better now. But we still ask the same question with the same doubts. Why do the innocent suffer? Perhaps we need to take Job's mind-blowing experience more seriously.

People can meet God and know his love. But that

does not protect them from suffering. They may have even more pain as a result. But there is a difference. God is there. He will help them overcome their suffering. They will learn to live with it. Job did – and look what happened to him!